D1576764

The Life and Work of...

Henri
Matisse

Paul Flux

www.heinemann.co.uk/library
Visit our website to find out more information about Heinemann Library books.

To order:

 Phone 44 (0) 1865 888066

 Send a fax to 44 (0) 1865 314091

 Visit the Heinemann Bookshop at www.heinemann.co.uk/library to browse our catalogue
and order online.

First published in Great Britain by Heinemann Library, Halley Court, Jordan Hill, Oxford OX2 8EJ, a division of Reed Educational and Professional Publishing Ltd. Heinemann is a registered trademark of Reed Educational and Professional Publishing Ltd.

OXFORD MELBOURNE AUCKLAND JOHANNESBURG BLANTYRE
GABORONE IBADAN PORTSMOUTH (NH) USA CHICAGO

Designed by Celia Floyd
Illustrations by Karin Littlewood
Originated by Ambassador Litho Ltd
Printed and bound in Hong Kong/China

ISBN 0 431 09218 4

06 05 04 03 02
10 9 8 7 6 5 4 3 2 1

British Library Cataloguing in Publication Data

Flux, Paul
   The life and work of Henri Matisse
   1. Matisse, Henri, 1869 – 1954
   2. Painters – France – Biography – Juvenile literature
   3. Painting – France – Juvenile literature
   I. Title II. Henri Matisse
   759.4

Acknowledgements

The Publisher would like to thank the following for permission to reproduce photographs: AKG: p26; Bridgeman Art Library: pp4, 7, 13, 16, Albright Knox Art Gallery, Buffalo, New York p5, Chapelle di Rosaire, Venice p25, Hermitage, St Petersburg, Russia p9, Phillips Collection, Washington p23, Pushkin Museum, Moscow p19, Scottish National Gallery of Modern Art, Edinburgh p21; Christies Images: p17; CNAC/MNAN/RMN: p15; Corbis: p12; Hulton Archive: pp8, 10; Magnum Photos: p28; Mary Evans Picture Library: p18; Succession H Matisse/DACS 2002: pp27, 29; Museum of Modern Art, New York, Mrs Simon Guggenheim Fund: p11.

Cover photograph (*Fall of Icarus*, Henri Matisse) reproduced with permission of Bridgeman Art Library.

Every effort has been made to contact copyright holders of any material reproduced in this book. Any omissions will be rectified in subsequent printings if notice is given to the Publisher.

Any words appearing in the text in bold, **like this**, are explained in the Glossary.

Contents

Who was Henri Matisse?

Henri Matisse was a French artist. His work is still very popular. He was one of the best painters of the 20th century.

Henri painted many different things in his life. This is one of his best known pictures. Henri loved to use bright colours and strong lines.

Music, 1939

Early years

Henri Matisse was born on 31 December 1869, on his grandfather's farm in France. At school he showed little interest in art. He left school in 1887 to study **law** in Paris.

In 1890, when he was 21, Henri became very ill. His mother bought him a box of paints to cheer him up. He used them to paint pictures like this one.

Still-Life with Books and Candle, 1890

Love and marriage

In 1892 Henri met Amélie Parayre. They fell in love. In 1894 Henri's first child was born. He and Amélie had two more children, and lived in Paris.

Henri and Amélie were married in 1898. Henri painted this picture of his wife many years later. He often used her as a **model** for his paintings.

Portrait of Madame Matisse, 1913

Teaching art

In 1907 Henri opened his own art school. It was very popular. He had to close it in 1911. This was because the 60 students took up too much of his time.

Henri tried using colour in new ways. He painted this picture of his own **studio**. This was unlike any painting he had ever done before!

Red Studio, 1911

In the USA

In 1913 Henri was asked to show his work in New York. Americans had rarely seen such **abstract** and colourful pictures. The paintings didn't look like anything in real life.

A lot of people in the USA did not like Henri's paintings. They thought his work was too bright and difficult to understand. In Chicago people burned a copy of one of his pictures. They were showing how much they disliked it.

Interior with Aubergines, 1911

War breaks out

In 1914 war began in Europe. Henri had many of his paintings hanging at an **exhibition** in Berlin. They were all taken by the German **government**.

14

Henri painted this picture after the war had begun. He wanted the darkness to show that war makes people frightened.

French Window at Collioure, 1914

Henri and Pablo Picasso

In 1918 Henri had a big **exhibition** with Pablo Picasso, another great artist. The two men painted quite differently, but they **admired** each other's work.

During the 1920s Henri grew more famous. He kept searching for better ways to paint. In 1925 he was given the Legion of Honour. This was a special award from the French **government**.

Woman Reading, 1922

Another war

In 1939 **World War II** began. Soon there were lots of German soldiers in France. Henri left Paris again and went back to live in southern France.

In 1939 Henri **separated** from Amélie, but he still thought about her. He was worried by the terrible war. The black background in this picture shows his troubled mood.

Still-Life with a Seashell on Black Marble, 1940

The war years

During the war Henri became very ill. He had to stay in bed for nearly a year. He was never in good health again.

This picture was finished when the war was at its worst. It shows the myth of **Icarus**, the man who flew too close to the Sun. Henri wanted to show how fighting could **destroy** fine ideas.

Jazz: Icarus, 1943

21

A troubled time

In April 1944 the German secret police **arrested** Henri's wife and daughter, Marguerite. They were sent to jail for helping the fight against the Germans. Henri was very worried about them.

Amélie and Marguerite were set free after many months in jail. Although he was worried and unwell, Henri continued to paint. For several years many of his paintings showed his fears for his family and country.

The Egyptian Curtain, 1948

The chapel at Vence

In 1947 Henri was visited by a nun. She had nursed him when he had been ill. She showed him a **design** she had made for a new church window. Henri decided to design a whole new **chapel**.

24

Henri took this work very seriously. It was four years before the chapel at Vence, in France, was finished. This is a window Henri designed for the chapel.

Tree of Life, 1951

Failing health

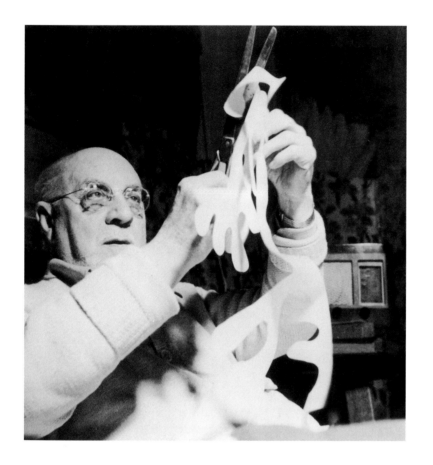

Soon Henri became too ill to paint anymore. He used **cut-out** pieces of coloured paper to make his pictures. Other people helped him. He found the results exciting and new.

Most of Henri's cut-outs show that life is enjoyable and full of fun. But some were made to show sadness, like this one of what an unhappy king sees.

Sorrows of the King, 1952

Last days

Henri continued to work although he was becoming very weak. He was working on a **design** for a church window when he died on 3 November 1954.

Henri used colour in ways no one had ever tried before. Even in his last works he **experimented** with bright colours, full of life. Henri was truly a great artist.

The Snail, 1953

Timeline

1869	Henri Matisse is born on 31 December, in northern France.
1887	Henri studies **law** in Paris.
1892	He begins to study painting in the **studio** of Gustave Moreau.
1898	Amélie Parayre and Henri are married. They travel to London and Corsica.
1904	Henri has his first one-man show.
1907	Henri opens his own art school in Paris. He meets Pablo Picasso for the first time.
1913	Henri shows his work in New York.
1914	Henri has paintings in an **exhibition** in Berlin. When war begins these paintings are taken by the German **government**.
1917	The artist Edgar Degas dies.
1918	Pablo Picasso and Henri hold a big exhibition together.
1927	Henri is given the painting prize at the Carnegie Exhibition.
1939	**World War II** breaks out.
1941	Henri is very unwell, but he returns to work.
1944	His wife and daughter are **arrested**.
1945	End of World War II.
1947	Henri begins work on the **chapel** at Vence.
1952	The Matisse Museum is set up at Henri's place of birth.
1954	Henri dies on 3 November.

Glossary

abstract   kind of art which does not try to show people or things. It uses shape and colour to make the picture.

admire   to think something or someone is very good

arrested   caught by the police

chapel   small part of a larger church, with its own altar

cut-out   piece of paper that has been cut into a shape

design   plan or drawing of something

destroy   break or ruin

exhibition   art on display for people to see

experiment   to try things out

government   people who control a country

Icarus   man in Greek myth who escaped from prison using wings his father had made. Icarus died when he flew too close to the Sun and the wax in his wings melted.

law   the rules of a country

model   someone who is drawn or painted by an artist

separated   split up, parted

studio   special room where an artist works

World War II   war fought in Europe, Africa and Asia from 1939 to 1945

More books to read

How Artists Use Shape, Paul Flux, Heinemann Library

Matisse, Getting to Know the World's Great Artists, Mike Venezia, Franklin Watts

More paintings to see

Notre-Dame, Henri Matisse, Tate Gallery, London

Studio under the Eaves, Henri Matisse, Fitzwilliam Museum, Cambridge

Index

Titles in the *Life and Work of* series include:

Hardback   0 431 09210 9

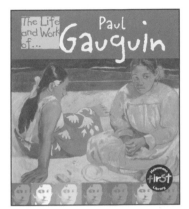

Hardback   0 431 09216 8

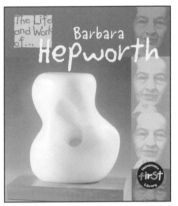

Hardback   0 431 09212 5

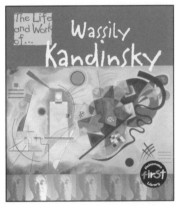

Hardback   0 431 09217 6

Hardback   0 431 09218 4

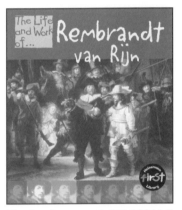

Hardback   0 431 09211 7

Hardback   0 431 09219 2

Find out about the other titles in this series on our website www.heinemann.co.uk/library